Saudade

First published 2019 by The Hedgehog Poetry Press

Published in the UK by
The Hedgehog Poetry Press
5, Coppack House
Churchill Avenue
Clevedon
BS21 6QW

www.hedgehogpress.co.uk

ISBN: 978-1-9160908-0-4

A CIP Catalogue record for this book is available from the British Library.

Saudade

by

Nigel Kent

for Kerry, Holly and Annie.

Contents

7.30 P.M. AT THE ARTS WORKSHOP

With iambs
beating loudly
in her chest
she stood to read
the lines which
she had drilled
to dance
with elegance and
grace.

Yet now
those naked words
shivered
on the page
and shuffled shyly
to the ledge
of every line,
where sense
tripped,
and sprawled
red-faced
into silent
space.

DE-PICT

He keeps his memories
contained in tubes
with caps twisted tight,
laid out in shades
from light to dark.

There they stay
unformed, unshaped
until those days
he minds to let them loose
to paint a picture of his past...
...a short-trousered boy
racing home late,
having lingered at school
too long, eyes aglow
with the callow hope that
she won't notice,

but there she stands,
at the garden gate,
on guard, her crowbar arms folded
across a bosom, tapped
of tenderness by his absent dad...

He pauses,

bristling with a lifetime's
fear and hate,

and then

with bold, decisive strokes,
he brushes her
away and covers
the brooding clouds
with a bright summer sky,

much too blue.

'NOT AN ORPHAN IN THE WHOLE WORLD CAN BE SO DESERTED AS A CHILD WHO IS OUTCAST FROM A LIVING PARENT'S LOVE'. (CHARLES DICKENS)

A prose poem

You slam the door   with all the might that you can muster,   as if the bang will bring her to her knees   and leave her in a bleeding heap.   You do not hear the doves,   scattering from your neighbour's roofs, climbing steeply,   wings slapping frantically,   as if fleeing from attack. You hear only her words that linger   like stale smoke upon your clothes: words that can't be wiped away   like the angry tears of snot hanging from your nose.   Words that blame and shame   which follow you to school, find echoes in seething corridors,   in felt tip pen on toilet doors,   in sighs and rolling eyes.   Until you rush home, trigger cocked,   to a door she's double-locked   which leaves you standing, helpless on the step, mocked on every side by her beloved columbines,   tongues poking out from pink-painted lips.   You shoot out a foot.   Again.   Again and again and again,   kicking the petals from their stems   which land upon the garden path   like the plump, bloodied breasts of returning doves blasted   from above.

WEEK-ENDING

On Friday nights at exactly five o'clock
she'd set the catch to make my father
knock: the rapid rap of knuckle on the wood
would drive her to the door, where with hand
held out she'd take the packet with his pay,
the ticket he must have to pass into his house.

Then she'd make him watch her count
the meagre sum he'd earned that week
and listen to her list the many promises
he'd made but failed to keep. Of course,
he'd heard it all before and slurs, which used
to sting like pellets shot at naked flesh,
would mostly miss their mark.

They'd used up all their words so long ago:
they'd nothing new to say and silence
fell too often like a freezing fog:
a bitter winter chill that would not
lift the whole weekend and last,
most likely, long into the week.

MAN-MADE

It should have been a day for bonding:
a dad and his lad at the County Ground,
though he'd had to insist the boy
pass up his beloved dance for once
for a chance to play before the game
with the bat and ball he'd bought.

The father bowls; the boy misses.
The father bowls; the boy misses.

No cajoling, no matter how loud, can make
the boy's limp bat meet moving ball
or still his quivering limbs that flinch
at every threat of bruising blows.
Bat discarded, they try some catches instead;
the boy's china fingers cupped in readiness.

The father throws, the boy misses.
The father throws, the boy misses.

Each time his son runs off, released,
to fetch the ball, gliding with an easy grace.
Balanced on tip-toes, feet turned out,
he floats across his father's boundary,
to return the ball in clumsy underarms,
that knock his father's hopes clean out the ground.

The father sighs, the boy says sorry.
The father sighs, the boy says sorry.

CURSED

In the corridor
he will not overtake
the hard boys
from the estate;
who'll spray
abuse at him
and though he'll rub
and scrub,
the stain
always remains,
marking him
the geek,
the freak,
who hides
in the darkest corner
of the school yard,
shivering with
the timid and the tense,
their backs
towards the fence,
invisible
to duty teachers,
who shield steaming tea
from misdirected missiles,
and wait for lessons
to begin again
in which he'll coast
in neutral
through the work they set.
The fast-lane learner
who never idles,
whilst the others
require push-starting.

The boy who has
the answer before
the question's asked.
The boy who knows
he's gifted
but believes
he's cursed.

OUT OF THE MOUTHS

My big brother's much brainier than me;
he passed the test for grammar school.
He knows how the wireless works:
he says it runs on waves: short, medium and long.
Sometimes when mum and dad are out
he moves the dial and lets me hear them swoosh.
But there's no sound today, I think it must be bust.
My brother says it was high tide last night
and a surge of salty water washed away its works.

POP-UP PRINCESS

She's a *'Hello'* girl, a scholar of celebrity,
student of the stars, who'd rather read
the A list than revise and lives her life
online garnering gossip from the famous.
She's the pop-up princess with glass slipper
dreams who's mastered the knee pop pose,
the curve enhancing stance, and the lip-stick pout,
captured in selfies that fill her Facebook daily.
This is the night she has planned for;
the night she's begged and bargained for;
the night her parents took a payday loan for.

Over too quickly in a photographer's flash,
when the flicker of fluorescent lights cannot be
rebuffed and ballroom becomes school hall again.
No choice but to drag herself home, leaving friends
behind with promises she knows she'll break.
Head down, she does not see the dew has stolen
her crown of golden curls and does not hear
the clink of crystals dropping from her dress
to mark her solitary passage through the dark.
Now, only tomorrow exists, when her mother
will insist she zip up her dreams in garment bags
and hang them in the wardrobe at the back,
next to the uniform she'll wear no more.

NORMAL

At midnight
his life begins.

They cannot hear
my scream scratching
the walls of senses too thin
to bear the weight
of truth:

life's gift, double wrapped,
suspended
by a thread, tight around
his misshapen head.

No time
for ceremonial cutting
of the chord,
as midwives rush
to fan the feeble
flicker of his heart.
and all anticipation
coagulates
in the antiseptic air.

    * * *

Now each day at three a.m.
I rise, sleep-heavy,
lumbering to his cot
as whimper turns to wail
and in the calm
of nursing time
I see
normal
in his spine's twist
normal
in his eyes' void
normal
in his limbs' twitch.

and wish
the world could see him
with a mother's eyes.

JULIET IN THE HIJAB

She'd promised them gangs,
riots in the streets, revenge:
Eastenders in Verona, she had said.
Even subsidised the costs to turn
the spot away from their estate
and focus eyes beyond the flats.

Act One, they cannot see beyond
men dressed in tights, swollen
codpieces, breasts squeezed
skyward by tight-fitting bodices,
and their titters rub away the age-thin
patience of matinee habitués.

Act Two, they launch a fresh attack
across the generation gap:
an armoury of drinks and snacks
that snap back disapproving heads,
assailed by bottles' snorts
and wrappers' insistent whispers.

Act Three, too much to bear their teacher
throws her hands up in despair,
and in the darkness pulls her pupils out.
They do not need cajoling, their yawns
are wide enough to swallow time:
all that is, save one, Jahidah.

She sees a sister on the stage,
who reaches out to take her hand
to tell a story she understands.
She sits wide-eyed, in her back-row seat,
and though there is no one around her,
she knows that she is alone no longer.

FRENCHAY, 1960

His mother parked him
opposite me, a young boy,
about my age: wearing
a black rubber helmet
and with limbs like buckled straws.
My father mouthed to me
to look away
and seek fascination
in the bland brick walls,
as the woman struggled
to contain her son's plaintive
wails that streamed like spittle
from his twisted lips.
But I was mesmerised
by the hypnotic nodding
of his head and by the brown,
unblinking eyes
that fixed on mine
and silently said, "Hi!"

MISCARRIED

When she lost the little girl she'd longed for,
they did not try again; 'Too old!' he'd said.
She did not lie silently in a closed-curtain room;
she did not stare mutely into the unused cot.

Her grief was a howling, bared-teeth grief;
a sinew-ripping grief; a snapping, snarling grief
that locked its jaws around her throat
and swiped at both his outstretched hands.

He learned in time to tip-toe round her,
flattening himself against the nursery walls,
but he never could ignore the quiet sound
of gnawing, as it devoured her hour by hour.

MAN OF WORDS

You were so different
from your older brother.
I'd toss words to you,
cajoling you to catch them
and throw them back.
But unlike him,
you would not play;
you'd let them fall
and watch them
bounce across the floor.
Silence was your mouthpiece;
but you were simply biding time,
storing the words
you let drop,
and snapping them together
with muffled clicks,
to make a labyrinth
of plastic streets
and towering houses,
where you would hide,
count to ten
and challenge me to find you,
though I never could,
not even when I cheated.
You made me wait,
testing patience till it failed.
Then you'd emerge
wearing expressions,
borrowed from friends,
concealing the face
I've never learned to read.

CASTING OFF

Today he strains to hold her in his hands,
like an angler struggling to control his catch.
The water's much too deep for one so young
and though she worms and twists and turns
she cannot slip the strictures of his fingers
hooked around her flailing limbs.

In time he knows he'll have to teach her how
to swim the open seas, to ride the tides,
to cruise the currents and find her course
in parlous waters, until one day he'll watch her
wade into its depths, leaving him to track
the choppy passage of her bathing cap,
wishing he could reel her in.

FOLLOWER

You'd follow us into the kitchen,
our four year-old interrogator,
more insistent than the Spanish Inquisition,
stretching patience on learning's rack,

pursuing your inquiries
with the zeal of a fanatic:
each question sparking forty more
and forty more again.

We tried to answer truthfully,
shunning myths of stork deliveries
and babies under gooseberry bushes,
when topics took a tricky turn.

Now you're a teenager,
you're a member of a silent order,
bowed at the breakfast table,
in daily devotions to the screen.

Your day prescribed by the summons
of pings and pokes, calling you
to the private communion of friends,
who find truths in tablets of plastic.

You're a headphone hermit,
devout celebrant of the selfie,
lost to an eternal life online,
where Google is God.

EMPTY NEST

I find it under
the cherry tree:
a starling's nest,
abandoned by its
rowdy residents
who took their leave
two weeks before,
writing farewell
in cursive script
across the pale,
vellum sky.

In cradled fingers
I take it to the house,
and lay it by
her pile of post:
something to show
and tell when she
returns at end of
term...

...which seems so
long to wait
and feelings that
I'd cased
and stored
with carrier bags
of cuddly toys
and old school books
strain the
catches.

I see her, still,
standing on
the hostel steps,
half-turned,
hand raised,
and her last
whispered bye
evaporating
from the clouded
glass
and remember how
returning home

I lost my way.

BREAKFAST SCENE

We watch her fill the glass
up to its brim with juice
and carry it like the sacrament,
across the busy breakfast room,
tongue pressed between her lips,
to where her mum will sit.

Her father shovels sugar
into a cup of cooling tea
to sweeten the bitterness
that has spiked their holiday;
the image of her with their friend
stirring, stirring, stirring.

The mother doesn't notice
what her child's prepared;
she's looking for her partner,
who, seeing her arrive, walks off,
wading through a churning sea, chin deep,
the sand sinking beneath his leaden feet.

'DADDY'S GOING, MUMMY!'
her daughter screams
and makes us silent extras
in this breakfast scene;
wishing we had lines to shape
a new direction to this plot.

His partner grabs the siren child
fighting sandaled feet
that kick out vainly at her fears,
and smash the love-filled glass instead,
which haemorrhages unchecked
across the pristine linen,

and though in seconds a waitress
removes the sodden cloth
and mops up the sticky dregs
dripping from the table top,
she cannot rid the room of the stain
the family has left behind.

FARAWAY

At seven she had not sent the text
she'd told him to expect at six.
He would have rung,
but his little girl's a woman
now, nearly twenty-five,
who hated him to fuss.

At eight and nine, his phone
remained resolutely mute
despite the many times
he entreated it to ping
or ring, and reason retreated,
speechless, from his side.

Thoughts till now suppressed
rose up: a rowdy insurrection
assailing him on every side:
of leather-coated kidnap gangs
of carnal bar-room boys,
of terrorists in tourist traps.

At ten, he conjured with
a hundred urgent prayers a net
he hoped would catch her fall.
A litany of promises,
traded for His solemn guarantee
that she'd be safe, secure.

As eleven turned to twelve
he drained the dregs of consolation
from the bottom of the glass,
and retreated defeated
into a restless sleep,
so that the words
he'd craved for arrived, unheard.

RED CANNA

after Georgia O'Keefe

This is no shy, modest flower
that seeks the solitude of shade:
this is a wild, wanton flower
swaying sensuously in the breeze,
drunk with the summer sun
that makes vivid, lewd proposals
to the workers, hovering in the garden,
who, seduced by the promise of her perfume,
enter in an ecstasy of nectar.

SAUDADE I

She takes them to be spots of light
reflected in the mirrors of her eyes,
like the specks of white a painter
knows sparks life into a subject's face.
Until she looks again to find
familiar features reflected back
that make synapses flash,
to light a memory,
sunshine sharp and bright,
concealed too long beneath
the fabric of a mother's lies.
A pale, drawn face
beneath the landing light,
lingering too long outside her open door,
as if he sensed were he to enter
one look would trip affection's wire
and send him crashing to his knees.
She watches him retreat, grabbing
his belongings in the bin bags at his feet,
regret already running down unshaven cheeks.
A memory, so hot and so intense,
it scorches a shadow on her eyes
that she'll see now at home, at work,
in every waking hour, in every room,
in every shop, in every crowded city street.

SAUDADE II

I return again,
stealing in unseen,
to scan your photographs
of melting ice-cream smiles,
of cloudless laughter,
of sunlit hugs and kisses,
and trace your features on the screen,
their form restoring
memories I thought
I could delete the day
I walked away...

...of your fractured face
framed in the window pane,
one arm tangled
in your mother's hair,
the other reaching out;
your open hand pressed
hard against the glass;
and the partisan wind
pulling at my rain-soaked coat...

I try once more
to cut and paste you
by my side
against a cropped summer sky
of saturated blue,
yet I cannot find a way
to place my arm
around your shoulders
and put my hand in
yours.

THE ROSE SHOE

after Walter Sickert

It was the shoe,
the damned shoe,
that did it!
Its pink, silk roses
and her exposed toes
roused thoughts
of wanton ways,
forbidden favours.
Impossible to ignore

Yet, she'd lain
stone-still throughout
head turned away,
hands in silent surrender,
letting the pleasure
I'd paid for
dribble away like the spittle
at the corners
of her gin-soaked lips.

I see her still,
as I rose to go,
flopping over,
face shrouded by hair,
and the viscid moonlight,
bleeding through
threadbare curtains,
that turned her flesh
the colour of butchered meat.

I hastened away
down the tenement stairs
as if pursued by police,
but there's no escape:
she infects
every oozing minute
like an open sore,
which I must hide
from my wide-eyed wife.

THE MAIDS

after Paula Rego

Our Mistress snaps
and slaps my hand,
to stop the brush
that wrestles with sleep's knots
in hair that smells
of cedarwood,
like the unseasoned logs
which father would
set upon the block
and split
with a single blow
to send them spinning
into the brambles' tangle,
where with threats and smacks
he'd force us to fetch them,
their sticky sap
violating hands.

I see his face in hers
caught in the mirror:
squatting on
the nursing chair,
forcing us to kneel:
a block of muscle,
frozen hard,
the threat of spreading legs,
stubby fingers
fumbling with pearl buttons
and a feeling, fierce and feral,
till then penned in,
charges through
time's dense brush
to the knotted fist,
raised above
my Mistress's head.

SEPARATION

after Edvard Munch

They tell me now it's time
to make a bonfire of the past
and warm the hands
that once were gloved in yours
against its healing flames.
Yet I cannot leave the lap
of your beloved chair
with its soft arms around me,
reading letters
you once wrote
that pile up memories
like bundles of old newspapers,
stacked from floor to ceiling,
so that friends must
skirt around them,
lest they bring the paper pillars
crashing to the ground,
burying me beneath.

IN THE CAR

after Roy Lichtenstein

They were school prom royalty,
red carpet perfection:
the quarterback and his drama star,
who could easily have been
Monroe's much prettier sister.
The day he walked her down the aisle
like a trophy he had won,
the envy of his friends resounded
loudly round the room.

His playbook played out perfectly
as long as he made the calls
and she admitted that she let him
as she'd been trained to act a part.
She wore the clothes he chose her,
cooked the food he said he liked,
and kept their home so spotless
he had no reason to find fault
with the wife whom he'd deposed.

When he picked her up that day
from a conference of friends
she fixed her eyes firmly
on the rugged road ahead
and recited a solemn soliloquy
that she'd rehearsed for weeks
prompted by the courage
she'd borrowed from the bottle,
hidden in her bag.

She talked of justice and equality
of a woman's right to choose,
of sexual harassment and sisterhood,
and the tyranny of high heels.
He watched anger and resentment
strip the powder from her face
to reveal a woman, he believed,
only a baby could sort out.

LIPSTICK SMILE

'You're settling
for second-hand',
my father said
between sips of scalding tea,
when I confessed
that my new girl still
carried on her back
the sadness of a past relationship.
'Listen, son,' he lectured,
'the tears and fears
which move you now,
are proof of damaged goods.
Don't believe
that all it needs
is love and care
to make a good repair.
That's like painting
over flakes of rust;
the past carries on
corroding unseen beneath.'
My mother listened
saying nothing,
then turned to the mirror
above the mantelpiece
to fix the lipstick smile,
slipping down her chin.

CHAMPAGNE AFTERNOONS

They lie locked together in their hotel room,
words deferring to the urgency of lips
and frenzied fingers searching for ecstasy,

the pressure of their passion building
till it uncorks a fizzing stream that flows
unchecked through every sense:

a delicious drunkenness that bubbles in
befuddled brains and leaves them drained
yet demanding more, more, more,

until she releases him reluctantly
to trudge home to a marriage
as flat and sour as last week's sparkling wine.

CLEARING OUT

We roused her from her bed
with our knocks and shouts.
She'd forgotten we were coming
to start upon the shed:
we'd been asked to clear the jumble,
there'd be no room for in the home.

She stood there in her nightie,
and monitored every move,
insisting she see each item
before we dumped it in the skip,
as if there were a danger
we'd ditch some priceless gem.

We found no Clarice Cliff,
no first editions in the books,
just objects wrapped in memories,
tied with nostalgia's string:
things she'd put aside
as *'Not yet ready for the tip!'*

She shared their stories with us
in words - so often frozen -
that flowed that day like years.
*'See this! My knitted swimsuit
I wore on honeymoon and that's
the broken wireless my father let me tune...'*

When at last the shed was empty,
the skip remained unfilled.
Her life lay firmly anchored
in the piles around her feet
and as we tried to move them,
she cried, *'Not yet! Not yet! Not yet!'*

DIGNITAS

Every day the beauty with the lilac,
latex gloves comes to shower him;
her blue plastic apron barely concealing
contours that no man could ignore.

Before, he might have made a pass
at her but since the stroke he chokes
on words that turn to pebbles in his
mouth and thoughts resist all calls

upstairs to rouse themselves from bed.
So there he stands before her. Naked.
Silent. Pale arms hanging flaccidly
at his sides, powerless to prevent

the daily trespass of her hands
that wash away his dignity, bit by bit,
like the dirt swirling and gurgling
down the drain beneath his feet.

RECOVERY

The shock of winter over,
he watched the colour
drain back into the garden.
The sun's soft fingers soothed
his irradiated cheeks, eased
the rawness of his blistered throat,
and raised him from the daybed;
his first few steps for weeks,
unsteady and determined
as a new-born lamb's.
He knew then a swallow
or two would follow.

SWEET AND SOUR

He carries his gratitude
in two frayed bags for life
filled with Kilner jars
of pickled strawberries.
A summer preserved,
for the winter
he wasn't sure he'd make
but useless now to a man
without a swallow
and who's lost all
sense of taste.
Today, they'll serve
as surrogates for words
that bled away unchecked
when they excised his voice
and though they say
they'll teach him soon
to talk again,
till then they must taste
his thanks in the berries'
sun-filled hearts
for a life
they have prolonged :
a life both
sweet and sour.

AUDREY'S TIME

We wheel her into
the waning evening sun
as if the sunlight
would somehow restore her
like some wilting plant.

She does not speak.
Not now.
Words run away
from her,
slipping her grasp
like unruly children,
reluctant to come home
at dusk.

We fill her time,
with family photos
till we have earned
our leave;
filial duty fulfilled
for yet another week.

She looks at
our departure
with shuttered eyes,
mouth ajar,
memories escaping
with every feeble wheeze,
whilst her tissue soft hands
clench and unclench
in her lap,
as if anticipating
some last
decisive assault,

which we think
guiltily
can't come
too
soon.

HOME TRUTHS

At dawn radios sing discordant songs,
to captive audiences of one,

interned in galleries of forgotten faces,
of fading children in silent playgrounds.

Here time's gears slip: each hour repeats,
stuck in a rhythm that will not cease:

every day Dorothy, by a flameless fire,
shares jigsaw memories with an empty chair;

Tom shells pistachios he never eats,
envious of the kernels he releases;

Elsie, seeing sleights in every smile,
hides behind the curtains, covering her eyes;

Jenny swigs brandy from a smuggled bottle,
swallowing minutes with each mouthful.

Till at last darkness shuffles down the hall,
its slippered feet pausing at every door.

Bringing sleep to stop the clock,
it turns the key, leaves the door unlocked.

THE BLIND MAGI

The decorations completed
and presents stacked
beneath the tree,
we stargazers brave
winter's bitter chill
to follow the promise
of the city's beacon-glow,
where a galaxy, suspended
above its teeming streets,
burns with a light so bright
it wipes out shadows
and bleaches sight white,
so we stumble star-blind
past the heap of blankets
twitching in the doorway
of the empty charity shop;
past the grey, forgotten face
fading at the window
of his first-floor flat;
past the single mother
squatting on the hostel steps,
her new-born baby
howling in her lap.

FITTING

I watch her wobble
along the pathway
on a bike one size too big:
tyres factory-fresh;
and paint the colour
of the bubble-gum
that flecks the fractured
pavement slabs.

On her chest
a plate-sized badge
shouts loudly
to the indifferent estate
that today she's celebrating
being eight.

Suddenly
a siren squeal
of brand-new brakes;
the prized bike
clatters
to the ground.

She staggers back
her head smacks tarmac;
eyes flicker
with a storm that rages
in a timeless surge
of tics and kicks
and flooded senses
that stream
from lips and hips.

And whilst
I wait,
at her side,
willing the ambulance
to arrive,
the silent street
pretends to sleep,
all finer feelings
roughened by poverty's
unrelenting rub
into a calloused skin
too hard for this girl's
suffering to soften.

So I am
not surprised
that when I leave,
relieved,
I see
her precious bike has

disappeared.

'WE ARE NOT FREE TO FOLLOW OUR OWN DEVICES' (CHARLES DICKENS)

You descend upon the factory floor   radiating the power of the zero hour.   Your workers know the fingers,   twitching in your pockets, itch for their stop switches,   so they'll always bear a smile   while you pause by their machines.   Though she's new   and you do not know her   you're certain she'll say **nothing**   when you call her by the word your wife abhors;   **nothing** when your breath toys with the curls on her bowed neck;   **nothing** when you place your hand upon her waist and run it up and down her back.   You'll leave your fingerprints behind: smears and smuts   set beneath the surface of the skin   that she'll conceal from family and friends,   like crude tattoos,   knowing she'll never find the hours   to have them removed.

STAFFROOM GUERRILLA

I lurk in the shadows at the back,
behind a barricade of unmarked books,
armed with an arsenal of incendiary remarks
to stop our new head teacher in her tracks.
The last pocket of resistance to her
classroom revolution that cannot
be conscripted to her cause.
I aim my asides with a sniper's
resolution, rejoicing at each falter
and each fall, always hoping
I'll succeed in securing her surrender
but knowing it's unlikely and I'll fail,
for she battles through each setback,
growing stronger with each skirmish,
supported by the quislings on the staff.
I can't deny the fact that soon she'll wipe me out,
as she does seditious scribbling on the board.
Thirty years just swept away by a troop
of willing cleaners with new brooms.

SLEIGHT OF HAND

He stands over me.

I cannot see his face
only the granite grey slacks,
the diamond shine
of patent shoes,
and the red, rolled banknote,
proffered casually
between two fingers
as though some cheap
cigarette.

Fifty pounds!

Street magic
that turns a troubled
night in doorways to
a hostel day
and the luxury of
a locked door...

...but for the scratch of a match...

and the magician's hand,
transformed,
teases the surface of the note
with an obdurate flame,
browning and blackening
fledgling hopes which

stall
        and
                crash
in a spiral of
smoke and ash.

He stands over me –
I see his face -
surveying the wreckage
from the height
of privilege,
before he takes off
and soars.

'BLEAK, DARK, AND PIERCING COLD, IT WAS A NIGHT FOR THE WELL-HOUSED AND FED TO DRAW ROUND THE BRIGHT FIRE, AND THANK GOD THEY WERE AT HOME; AND FOR THE HOMELESS STARVING WRETCH TO LAY HIM DOWN AND DIE.' (CHARLES DICKENS)

A prose poem

They spit you out   like gum that's lost its taste,   yet they complain it's you   who litters the city's streets.   Every day you squat upon a cardboard mat   with paper cup to catch the coins   you hope   might drop from pockets picked by pity.   Later you shelter in the canvas town that rises beneath the railway arches,   where you unpack those thoughts   you'd like to put away for good: of friends fallen on foreign sands,   of a sickness that can't be seen,   of a wife who couldn't feel your pain,   so you cannot sleep again.   That tune, you used to like,   spins round and round your head,   but now it's played in minor chords,   on a guitar always one string short;   a tune the politician, hurrying past, has never heard.   He's late for the train returning to the Shire,   irked by the sticky glob embedded in the tread of handmade shoes   which he'd rather throw away   than take the time to clean.

THE URBAN SHAMAN

He sways upon the stage,
hand above his head
drumming the rhythm
of the poem on the page
and throwing words
like holy bones,
to summons spirits to the room.

An oily opalescence,
clothed in clouds of fumes
that stink of Soho's streets,
morphs before us
into a city of a thousand
cuts laid bare:
her sleeves ripped back
to show the weeping wounds
that she conceals,
where blades have failed
to lance the pain
or excise memories
of bailiffs banging at her door
to serve her notice on her past
and leave her standing on the landing
with her future
in five supermarket bags.

He finishes the poem,
claps together
the covers of the book,
yet still the spirits
fill the air
and we feel
the tug of fingers
on our arms
forcing us
to linger, linger, linger.

ACKNOWLEDGEMENTS

With thanks to the editors of the following publications in which some of these poems first appeared:
A Restricted View from Under the Hedge, The Road to Clevedon Pier, South Magazine, Poems for Keeps, What the Elephant said to the Peacock, the Poetry Association of the Open University anthologies, Acumen, Eyeflash Poetry, and *Persona non Grata.*

I am also grateful to Stephen Belinfante, John Prangnell, Robin Evans, Dave Griffin and Mike Dowling for their encouragement and to Nick Browne for the cover and portrait photograph.

Last but not least, a special thanks to Mark Davidson, whose enthusiasm for new writing made this possible and to Maggie Sawkins, Isabelle Kenyon and Adrian Green for agreeing to comment on the manuscript!